34880000 823281

BOOK CHARGING CARD

Accession No. _____ Call No. 976.1 NAU

Author Nault, Jennifer

Title New Jersey

Date

976.1 NAU.

Nault, Jennifer

New Jersey

34880000 823281

NEW JERSEY

Jennifer Nault

Published by Weigl Publishers Inc.
123 South Broad Street, Box 227
Mankato, MN   56002
USA
Web site: http://www.weigl.com

Library of Congress Cataloging-in-Publication Data

Nault, Jennifer.
New Jersey / Jennifer Nault.
p. cm. -- (A kid's guide to American states)
Includes index.
ISBN 1-930954-48-4
1. New Jersey--Juvenile literature. [1. New Jersey.] I. Title. II. Series.

F134.3 .N38 2001

2001017994

ISBN 1-930954-91-3 (pbk.)

Printed in the United States of America
1 2 3 4 5 6 7 8 9 10   05 04 03 02 01

Project Coordinator
Michael Lowry
Copy Editor
Bryan Pezzi
Designers
Warren Clark
Terry Paulhus
Layout
Susan Kenyon
Photo Researcher
Diana Marshall

Photograph Credits

CONTENTS

The Great Falls National Historic Industrial Site is home to some of the largest early manufacturing plants in the country.

INTRODUCTION

New Jersey is a delightful state to call home. It offers its citizens a rich blend of fascinating cultures, diverse land regions, and thriving economic activities. New Jersey is nicknamed "The Garden State" for its early farming days. The state was once the main supplier of fresh fruits and vegetables for major cities like New York and Philadelphia.

New Jersey has a long tradition of scientific, industrial, and technological creativity. In fact, the well-known scientist Albert Einstein spent the last years of his life working at New Jersey's Princeton University. The state was also the site of inventor Thomas Edison's residence and his laboratory. Edison is known for inventing the phonograph, the telephone, and the light bulb. Edison and many others have helped New Jersey become a world leader in technology and communications.

QUICK FACTS

The name "New Jersey" comes from the island of Jersey in the English Channel. The island was the birthplace of Sir George Carteret, one of the **proprietors** of New Jersey during the late-1600s.

New Jersey adopted the horse as its state animal in 1977.

New Jersey's state flag has a beige background. The state's coat of arms is attached to a horse's neck in the center. On either side is a goddess. One represents liberty, the other agriculture.

The phonograph was invented in Thomas Alva Edison's laboratory in West Orange.

The terminal building for the Central Railroad of New Jersey was built in 1889. Today, the terminal is part of Liberty State Park.

QUICK FACTS

Before the invention of the automobile, it took horse-drawn wagons five days to bring passengers from New York City, through New Jersey, to Philadelphia. Thanks to automobiles and fast highways, this 90-mile journey now takes less than two hours.

The PATH railroad system links New Jersey and New York across the Hudson River. It carries more than 50 million passengers per year.

New Jersey has the most densely packed system of highways and railroads in the nation.

Getting There

New Jersey is located in the central-Atlantic region of the United States. The state is bordered by Delaware Bay to the south, Pennsylvania to the west, New York to the north, and the Atlantic Ocean to the east. New Jersey's coastal location makes it an important arrival point for cargo ships, ocean vessels, and freighters.

New Jersey has long been an important transportation route between New York City and Philadelphia. New Jersey **commuters** can access New York City by driving over the George Washington Bridge or through the Lincoln and Holland tunnels. There are four bridges that link New Jersey to Philadelphia. The New Jersey Turnpike, one of New Jersey's principal highways, and part of Interstate 95, spans 132 miles. The state's major airports are located in Newark, Teterboro, and Pomona.

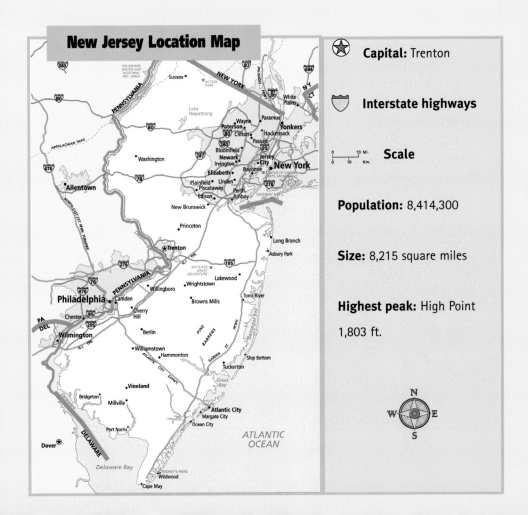

New Jersey Location Map

Capital: Trenton

Interstate highways

Scale

Population: 8,414,300

Size: 8,215 square miles

Highest peak: High Point 1,803 ft.

Visitors to the Old Barracks Museum in Trenton can witness the re-enactment of battles from the American Revolution.

New Jersey is rich in history. In the mid-1600s, the Dutch, British, and Swedish struggled for control of the region. During the American Revolution, more than 100 battles were fought on New Jersey soil and about 17,000 New Jersey citizens took up arms against the British. Two very important battles were fought in New Jersey—the Battle of Trenton and the Battle of Princeton. In the 1800s, New Jersey became an important transportation center. This allowed **industrialization** to spread across the state at a rapid pace.

New Jersey was one of the earliest states to join the Union. It entered on December 18, 1787, making it the third state to join, after Delaware and Pennsylvania. Three years later, Trenton was named the state capital.

QUICK FACTS

Trenton is named after New Jersey's first chief justice, William Trent. In 1784 and in 1799, Trenton acted as a temporary capital for the United States.

New Jersey's state motto is "Liberty and Prosperity."

In 1971, Kenneth Gibson became the first African-American mayor of Newark.

New Jersey's state flower is the fragrant purple violet.

The Clinton Historical Museum houses a restored 18th-century gristmill. The museum also features a country village with a blacksmith shop, schoolhouse, general store, and log cabin.

With more than 270,000 citizens, Newark is the most populated city in New Jersey.

QUICK FACTS

One of the worst disasters in **aviation** history occurred at Lakehurst when the *Hindenburg* airship exploded on May 6, 1937, killing thirty-six people.

Samuel Morse sent the first successful telegraph message in the United States from Morristown in 1838. The message was sent 2 miles and read, "Railroad cars just arrived, 345 passengers."

New Jersey's cities are bustling with activity. Newark, located only 10 miles west of New York City, is the financial, trade, and transportation center of the state. Newark's population is as diverse as its industries. African Americans comprise more than half of the city's population. There are also many people of Italian, Portuguese, and Puerto-Rican descent. With such a large range of ethnic backgrounds, the state is as rich in culture as it is in commerce.

New Jersey has a large population—it ranks ninth in the nation. Incredibly, it is also the fifth-smallest state in the United States. This means that most neighborhoods are densely populated. While most residents live in cities, New Jersey's Atlantic coast offers a quick getaway for vacationers. The sand and surf attract many people to the shoreline, especially during summer months. Coastal Atlantic City beckons visitors with its 6-mile boardwalk, live entertainment, and amusement-park rides.

New Jersey has more than fifty resort areas. Some of the most well-known resorts in the United States can be found in New Jersey, such as Atlantic City, Cape May, Seaside Heights, and Avon-By-The-Sea.

The Delaware Water Gap is a "gap" in the Appalachian Mountains, through which the Delaware River flows.

LAND AND CLIMATE

Although New Jersey is a highly **urbanized** state, it still contains a wide variety of natural habitats. The state is made up of four land regions, which range from mountainous to marshy. The Appalachian Ridge and Valley region sprawls across the northwest corner of the state. The state's highest peak, High Peak, can be found here. It stands 1,803 feet above sea level.

Much of the New England Upland region is composed of gneiss, a hard rock that is formed under intense heat and pressure. The Piedmont region, in the east, is largely made up of carrot-red sandstone. To the south, the Atlantic Coastal Plain covers three-fifths of New Jersey.

In the summer, tropical air currents from the ocean can result in hot and humid conditions. The average temperature in July ranges from 70° Fahrenheit in the north to 76°F in the southwest. In January, mild ocean currents moderate the climate keeping the average temperature at a balmy 33°F.

Salt marshes along the state's coastal plain attract birds such as the egret.

NATURAL RESOURCES

Coastal waters and inland lakes supply New Jersey's fishing industry with hard clams, squid, skates, mackerels, and herrings. Lobster, scallop, and tuna are in danger of being overfished, and as a result are carefully managed.

During the American Revolution, northern New Jersey was an important source of iron ore. Today, only a few minerals are still mined in the state. The most important of these is basalt, followed by sand, gravel, and clay. While most of the trees in New Jersey are too small to be used for lumber, some are used to make wood pulp.

Natural resources no longer play an important role in New Jersey's economy. While early settlers once relied on the state's soils for a living, today less than 1 percent of New Jersey's residents farm the land. When industrialization spread across New Jersey in the nineteenth century, manufacturing replaced raw materials as the state's main source of income.

New Jersey's Pesticide Control Program works to protect the state's wildlife by monitoring chemicals in the environment.

QUICK FACTS

The oak is the most common tree in the northern New Jersey forests. The state's oak trees were once used in shipbuilding.

In 1970, the Department of Environmental Protection was formed. The department is responsible for conserving plants and animals in New Jersey, as well as maintaining water supplies.

Small quantities of oil and natural gas have been discovered off the coast of New Jersey.

New Jersey's fishing industry brings in about $100 million each year.

The Kittatinny Valley State Park is New Jersey's newest state park. It was created in 1994.

PLANTS AND ANIMALS

Forests cover nearly two-fifths of New Jersey. Woodlands in the northern part of the state contain hickory, oak, red maple, and hemlock trees. Less hardy trees grow closer to the Atlantic Coastal Plain. These include scrub oak, pitch pine, and white cedar. Many flowers flourish in the state, including honeysuckles, goldenrods, azaleas, buttercups, and Queen Anne's lace.

New Jersey is home to many different kinds of animals, including otters, muskrats, opossums, rabbits, deer, minks, skunks, and raccoons. Although they were quite scarce, black bears and coyotes are once again common to New Jersey.

QUICK FACTS

Migrating birds may find sanctuary at the Edwin B. Forsythe National Wildlife Refuge.

Island Beach, a state park, has over 3,000 acres of plant and animal life. The park is known for its sandy coastal dunes and tidal marshes.

The Marine Mammal Stranding Center saves stranded dolphins, sea turtles, porpoises, and seals.

It is estimated that between 1,000 and 1,500 coyotes roam the wooded and grassy areas of New Jersey.

New Jersey is home to the largest hawk migration in North America. About one quarter-of-a-million hawks migrate through the state every fall.

QUICK FACTS

New Jersey's state bird is the eastern goldfinch. This little, yellow bird will sometimes remain in New Jersey throughout the winter.

The red oak is New Jersey's state tree. It was adopted in 1950.

Despite its small size, New Jersey has 113 toxic-waste dumps—more than any other state.

New Jersey's natural areas attract many species of birds. Near the shores of the Atlantic Ocean, wild ducks and geese are common. Heading inland, hawks, ruffed grouse, quails, wild turkeys, partridges, and pheasants live in the forests and meadows. Rare birds can be found at the Cape May Bird Observatory. This facility is one of the top ten bird-watching spots in North America.

In the second half of the twentieth century, environmental problems threatened some of the state's diverse plant and animal life. As New Jersey's population grew, urban areas began to swallow up agricultural and wilderness areas. In addition, some of New Jersey's toxic-waste sites leaked pollutants into the ground water and soil. In the early 1990s, the government passed laws that helped to reduce the amount of toxic chemicals released into the environment.

Horseshoe crabs are often called "living fossils." Fossil records show that similar species of horseshoe crabs were living nearly 250 million years ago.

TOURISM

Atlantic City is known as "America's Favorite Playground."

With numerous resorts strung along the Atlantic coastline, tourism plays an important role in New Jersey's economy. Atlantic City is one of New Jersey's most popular attractions. This family resort is known for its sandy beaches lined with wooden boardwalks, amusement-park rides, carnivals, hotels, and gambling casinos.

Many New Jersey cities contain historic buildings and majestic homes, which date back to the eighteenth century. Visitors can step back in time in Trenton. Here, tourists may tour the William Trent House. This National Historic Monument is the oldest home in the city.

Visitors to West Orange can learn about science at Thomas Edison's laboratory. Now a national historic site, the laboratory remains exactly as Edison left it. Some of Edison's inventions at West Orange include the motion-picture camera, the phonograph, and the nickel-iron alkaline electric storage battery.

Visitors can tour Thomas Edison's machine shop in West Orange. Edison claimed that his machine shops could "build anything from a lady's watch to a Locomotive."

QUICK FACTS

The first boardwalk in the world was built in Atlantic City in 1870.

While most people associate the famous Statue of Liberty with New York, it is actually located on the New Jersey side of the Upper New York Bay.

Lucy the Elephant, a gigantic elephant constructed in the late 1800s, guards Margate Beach. Lucy was made out of wood and then covered with sheet metal.

New Jersey's manufacturing industry brings twenty-five times more money into the state than farming, mining, fishing, and forestry combined.

INDUSTRY

In the eighteenth century, many New Jersey industries specialized in leather tanning, glass blowing, and iron forging. In the following century, the production of heavy machinery, silk, cotton, clothing, and shoes helped fuel New Jersey's economy. The state's coastal location and its numerous railroad systems and steamboats transformed New Jersey into an important industrial center. Recently, New Jersey has become a leader in technology, communications, and research.

New Jersey's agricultural sector grows greenhouse and nursery products such as roses and lilies. New Jersey's main field crops are soybeans, corn, and hay. Cranberries thrive in the marshlands of the Atlantic Coastal Plain. Cranberry farmers flood their fields with water and use a water reel to shake off the ripened berries. They can then collect the floating berries into trucks. This method of harvesting cranberries is called "wet picking."

New Jersey is the third-largest producer of cranberries in the nation.

GOODS AND SERVICES

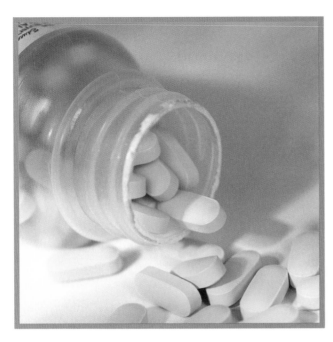

Pharmaceutical companies contribute more than $10 billion to New Jersey's economy.

New Jersey is the country's leading producer of chemicals and **pharmaceuticals**. The state has earned the nickname of "the nation's medicine chest," since about one-sixth of all medicines manufactured in the United States come from the state. Well-known pharmaceutical companies such as Johnson & Johnson, Merck, and Bristol-Myers Squibb are based in New Jersey. Other important goods that come from the state are machinery, instruments, clothing, and electrical products.

The service industry employs 33 percent of New Jersey's workers. Jobs in the service industry include working in hotels, banks, and restaurants. The majority of jobs in tourism are concentrated in the resorts on the Atlantic coast.

QUICK FACTS

New Jersey's pharmaceutical industry employs more than 140,000 people.

New Jersey was home to the first drive-in movie theater in the country. It was built in 1933.

In 1883, Roselle became the first town in the United States to receive electricity.

New Jersey is a leader in containerization. This means that ships, trains, trucks, and airplanes use containers to ship goods.

More than 33 million people visit Atlantic City every year.

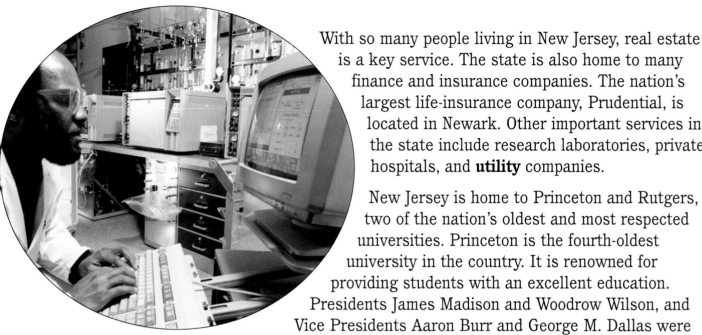

Many New Jersey research laboratories work closely with the state's universities and colleges.

With so many people living in New Jersey, real estate is a key service. The state is also home to many finance and insurance companies. The nation's largest life-insurance company, Prudential, is located in Newark. Other important services in the state include research laboratories, private hospitals, and **utility** companies.

New Jersey is home to Princeton and Rutgers, two of the nation's oldest and most respected universities. Princeton is the fourth-oldest university in the country. It is renowned for providing students with an excellent education. Presidents James Madison and Woodrow Wilson, and Vice Presidents Aaron Burr and George M. Dallas were all educated at Princeton. Rutgers is the eighth-oldest university in the country and enrolls more than 48,000 students each year. The university employs about 2,600 people on three campuses across the state.

QUICK FACTS

New Jersey is a constant leader in communications. The first interstate long-distance phone call was between New Jersey and New York in 1877. The first coast-to-coast telephone system originated in New Jersey, and the first satellite to broadcast live television across the Atlantic Ocean was designed in New Jersey.

About 240 newspapers are published in the state of New Jersey.

Many children in New Jersey must wear a uniform to school. About 17 percent of children attend private schools.

The headquarters for the Boy Scouts of America is in New Brunswick.

Princeton University was chartered in 1746 as the College of New Jersey. It was located in Elizabeth for one year, and then moved to Newark for nine, before it moved to its present location in 1756.

The primary Paleo-Indian hunting tool was the dart, which could easily be thrown as far as 300 feet.

FIRST NATIONS

New Jersey's first inhabitants lived in the area as long ago as 10,500 BC. **Archeologists** have named these people the Paleo-Indians. They are thought to have hunted large mammoths and other **prehistoric** animals. The Paleo-Indians were followed by the Archaic culture in 7,000 BC. The Archaic culture hunted deer and birds, and gathered plants.

By the 1500s, the Delaware were farming in the region. The Delaware lived in huts made of young saplings and covered in tree bark. They are known for using ashes from burned trees as **fertilizer** to help crops grow. With the arrival of European explorers and settlers, new diseases devastated the Delaware community. Without **immunity** to European diseases, many Delaware died. By the nineteenth century, most of the remaining Delaware had left New Jersey.

The Delaware ate berries, corn, squash, nuts, herbs, wild game, and fish.

A replica of the *Half Moon* was built in 1989. The original ship was used by Henry Hudson to explore the New Jersey area.

EXPLORERS AND MISSIONARIES

John Cabot was the first European to see the New Jersey coast in 1498. Cabot was an Italian **navigator** and explorer who was funded by the British. It was not until 1524 that the coast was explored and charted by Giovanni da Verrazzano. Verrazzano was an Italian explorer who sailed to North America under the French flag.

In 1609, a Dutch-owned ship called the *Half Moon* carried the English explorer Henry Hudson and his sailors to New Jersey. Although Verrazzano was the first to map the area, these Europeans were the first to set foot on New Jersey's soil. Henry Hudson explored the land for the Dutch, and soon Dutch settlements began to spring up across the state.

QUICK FACTS

Early explorers called the New Jersey region "the northeast territory."

New Jersey's Cape May is named after the Dutch explorer, Cornelius May. He sailed down the Delaware River in 1614.

Catholic missionaries arrived in New Jersey as early as 1672.

Henry Hudson thought that he had found a passageway between the Atlantic and Pacific Oceans when he sailed up the Hudson River. The river was named after him.

John Cabot claimed the New Jersey area for Britain in 1498.

EARLY SETTLERS

The New Sweden Farmstead Museum houses a reproduction of a seventeenth century Swedish log cabin.

In the early to mid-1600s, the Dutch West India Company claimed areas of New Jersey for the colony of New Netherland. The Swedish also established trading posts in the region. Both Dutch and Swedish traders grew rich through fur trading. In 1655, the Swedish traders were driven out by the Dutch.

In 1664, the British claimed the area for themselves. The British based their claim on the earlier voyage of Cabot, and backed it up with their mighty naval forces. The Dutch surrendered New Netherland to the British without a fight. Dutch settlers were allowed to stay, and all settlers were given political and religious freedom. The British re-named the region New Jersey, and began to sell off land to settlers at low prices. These policies attracted many new settlers to New Jersey.

Allaire Village was once an iron-mining community of over 400 people. Today, costumed guides help to re-create a part of New Jersey's past.

QUICK FACTS

The Dutch built a trading post in what is now Jersey City in 1618.

The New Jersey colony exchanged hands several times. After the British took the land from the Dutch in 1664, King Charles II gave it to his brother James, duke of York. Next, the duke of York gave the land to Lord John Berkeley and Sir George Carteret.

In New Jersey, Swedish settlers built the first log cabin in the United States.

By the 1690s, English, Scottish, Welsh, and Irish Quakers had settled in West Jersey. Quaker farms spread across the countryside.

Both Trenton, the state capital, and Princeton began as Quaker settlements.

QUICK FACTS

From 1676 to 1702, New Jersey was split in two, forming East Jersey and West Jersey. East Jersey was headed by Sir George Carteret, while West Jersey was run by the Quakers.

An ironworks plant, built in 1676 in Shrewsbury, sparked the industrial revolution in New Jersey.

During the American Revolution (1775-1783), George Washington and his troops spent several winters camped at Morristown.

North America's first Quaker colony settled in the western half of New Jersey in 1674. The Quakers, led by Edward Byllynge, bought West Jersey from Lord John Berkeley and made their home there. The Quakers were a religious group who rejected traditional forms of worship and relied instead upon silent meditation. They followed a simple life and wore plain clothing. Founded in England, the Quakers were often **persecuted** for their beliefs.

When the Quakers arrived in New Jersey, they were relieved to find a place where they could practice their religion freely. Different groups looking for religious and political freedom soon followed. In the late 1600s, Puritans, Baptists, Scottish, Welsh, and Irish groups settled in the New Jersey area. Many early settlers lived a **rural** farming life.

Cold Spring Village is a historic outdoor museum dedicated to preserving the lifestyles, trades, arts, crafts, and construction of early New Jersey rural life.

Jersey City, in northeastern New Jersey, is home to more than 232,000 people.

POPULATION

More than 8 million people live in New Jersey, making it the ninth most populated state in the country. The state's average **population density** is 1,134 people per square mile, which is the highest in the country. The average population density for the nation is 77 people per square mile. About 90 percent of the people in New Jersey live in urban areas. About three-quarters of the population lives in northern New Jersey, within a 30-mile radius of Manhattan Island. The largest cities in the state are Newark, Jersey City, and Paterson.

African Americans make up 13.6 percent of the state's population. Another 9.3 percent are of Puerto-Rican or Cuban origin, while 5.7 percent are Asian. About 71 percent of the state's citizens are of European descent.

The Portugal Day Festival, held every June in Newark, attracts close to 300,000 people to the Portuguese community of Ironbound.

New Jersey's state seal, seen here in the Capitol, was adopted in 1777.

Woodrow Wilson, who later became president of the United States, was elected as New Jersey's governor in 1910. He is remembered for protecting the rights of workers. He also passed laws forbidding companies from hiring young children.

New Jersey is represented in the United States government by two senators and thirteen members of the House of Representatives.

In 1967, and again in 1968, riots erupted across New Jersey. Many African Americans were frustrated with the poor conditions of the inner cities. As a result, commissions were set up to deal with problems in inner-city communities.

POLITICS AND GOVERNMENT

In New Jersey's early days, only those who owned land were allowed to hold positions in government. Landowners were called "freeholders." People who did not own land had very few rights. Today, county governments are called "boards of chosen freeholders" and are elected to three-year terms. Citizens no longer have to own land to hold government positions.

The state government is divided up into three branches—the executive, the legislative, and the judicial. The judicial branch is made up of the court system, while the executive branch is responsible for carrying out the laws. The executive branch is led by the governor, who is elected through a direct vote. The legislative branch consists of the Senate, which has forty members, and the General Assembly, which has eighty members. The legislature is responsible for creating laws.

New Jersey's State Capitol, in Trenton, has stained-glass windows, a breathtaking rotunda, and a 145-foot dome.

CULTURAL GROUPS

The annual Puerto Rican Day Parade in Paterson is a celebration of the heritage, culture, and arts of Puerto Rico.

New Jersey is home to a wide range of cultural groups. After the American Civil War, many people from overseas settled in the state. The majority came from Italy, England, and Ireland. Today, many of their **descendants** still live in the New Jersey area.

More than 1 million Latin Americans live in New Jersey. The state has the seventh-highest population of Latin Americans in the country. Latin Americans celebrate their culture in September during Hispanic Heritage Month. In the first week of September, Atlantic City hosts the Festival Latino Americano, which showcases Latin jazz music and salsa music. Flamenco dancers are also on hand to demonstrate their traditional dancing skills and costumes.

More than 25,000 people attend Atlantic City's Festival Latino Americano to take in Hispanic culture and arts.

QUICK FACTS

Flamenco dancing involves intricate stepping patterns and sweeping motions.

Many well-known African Americans grew up in New Jersey. Among them are Sarah Vaughan, a talented jazz singer, and Jessye Norman, an opera star.

The Powhatan Renape Nation, in Burlington County, educates people about the beliefs, traditions, and culture of the area's Native Americans.

Sammy Davis Jr. is one of the many well-known African Americans who visited Chicken Bone Beach.

QUICK FACTS

In the 1960s, living conditions became worse in many of New Jersey's urban centers. African-American leaders were inspired by the civil rights movement to start anti-poverty programs in their own communities. Many new political leaders from the African-American community rose to power during this time.

Atlantic City's African-American History Museum examines the city's African-American culture throughout the twentieth century.

Hackensack is home to one of the most important jazz-recording studios of all-time. Rudy Van Gelder set up a studio in his parents' living room and went on to record the sounds of such jazz greats as Miles Davis and John Coltrane.

African-American culture plays an important role in New Jersey's history. Some of the state's churches and businesses once served as hideouts for runaway slaves on the **Underground Railroad**. In 1926, Lawnside became the state's first entirely African-American municipality. Salem is home to one of the oldest African-American **congregations** in the country, which dates back to 1800.

African Americans also helped to develop New Jersey's rich coastal heritage. Atlantic City is home to Historic Chicken Bone Beach, the only Atlantic City beach that African Americans were allowed to use from 1900 to the 1950s. While the beach was created as a result of racial **segregation**, it came to represent African-American unity, and has been made into a historic site. The beach hosted giant celebrations with live jazz music and packed picnic-basket lunches. The beach got its name from the remains of pan-fried chicken lunches that were eaten on the beach.

Jazz legend Miles Davis recorded at Van Gelder's home studio in Hackensack.

David Copperfield was the youngest person ever to be admitted into the Society of American Magicians.

ARTS AND ENTERTAINMENT

For fans of music and the arts, New Jersey has numerous theaters, museums, concert halls, and opera houses. In 1997, the New Jersey Performing Arts Center opened in Newark. It is the sixth-largest arts center in the United States. The center is home to the New Jersey Symphony Orchestra, which entertains listeners with the sounds of classical music.

Magician David Copperfield comes from New Jersey. At the age of 12, he was admitted into the Society of American Magicians. Since then, Copperfield has performed many amazing tricks, such as escaping from a flaming raft over Niagara Falls and walking through the Great Wall of China.

QUICK FACTS

The New Jersey State Museum in Trenton is home to a 150-seat planetarium. The museum also houses art, science, and history exhibits.

One of Atlantic City's most popular events is the Annual Miss America Pageant, which began in 1921. Each fall, a winner is crowned with a tiara and becomes a national celebrity for a year.

Celebrities such as the Gipsy Kings, Placido Domingo, and George Winston have performed at the New Jersey Performing Arts Center.

Dance groups, such as the Alvin Ailey American Dance Theater, perform at the New Jersey Performing Arts Center.

Jack Nicholson is well known for his portrayal of Batman's arch-enemy the Joker in the 1989 movie *Batman*.

Many notable musicians, performers, and writers have called New Jersey home. Smooth-voiced singer Frank Sinatra was born in Hoboken in 1915. Sinatra charmed the world with his famous renditions of jazz ballads and show tunes, including "New York, New York."

Academy Award winners Meryl Streep and Jack Nicholson both come from New Jersey. Also from New Jersey are John Travolta, Joe Pesci, and Denzel Washington. Both Joe Pesci and Denzel Washington have won Academy Awards in the best supporting actor category.

Famous writers from New Jersey include poets Walt Whitman and William Carlos Williams, as well as writer Judy Blume. Judy Blume has written many humorous and honest novels for young people, including *Are You There God, It's Me Margaret* and *Otherwise Known as Sheila the Great*.

The Six Flags Great Adventure and Wild Safari, in Jackson, has the world's largest drive-through safari outside of Africa.

QUICK FACTS

Visitors to the Walt Whitman House and Cultural Museum can see some of the poet's early letters and poems.

Singer and songwriter Bruce Springsteen was born in Freehold. Springsteen sang about New Jersey on many of his albums, including *Greetings from Asbury Park*.

Animal lovers may experience an African safari at Six Flags Great Adventure and Wild Safari. Over 1,200 exotic animals can be seen on this drive-through safari.

SPORTS

New Jersey is credited with hosting the first organized baseball game.

New Jersey has much to offer fans of professional sports. The state is home to the New Jersey Nets, its professional basketball team, and the New Jersey Devils, its professional hockey team. The New Jersey Devils have brought home the Stanley Cup on two occasions, once in 1995 and again in 2000.

Both the New Jersey Nets and the New Jersey Devils play regularly in the state's main stadium, the Meadowlands Sports Complex. New York's two professional football teams, the New York Giants and the New York Jets also call the Meadowlands Sports Complex home. Located in East Rutherford, the Meadowlands Sports Complex hosts a variety of sporting events. Sports lovers can watch horse racing, professional football, hockey, and basketball at this venue.

QUICK FACTS

Shaquille O'Neal, a popular National Basketball Association (NBA) star, grew up in Newark.

Baseball legend Yogi Berra was born in Montclair. Berra's impressive career with the New York Yankees made him a national treasure.

Hoboken hosted the first organized baseball game in 1846. The New York Nine beat Alexander Cartwright's Knickerboxer club by a score of 23 to 1. Baseball historians refer to the event as "the day baseball was born." The game was held at Elysian Fields.

The first professional game of basketball was played in Trenton in 1896.

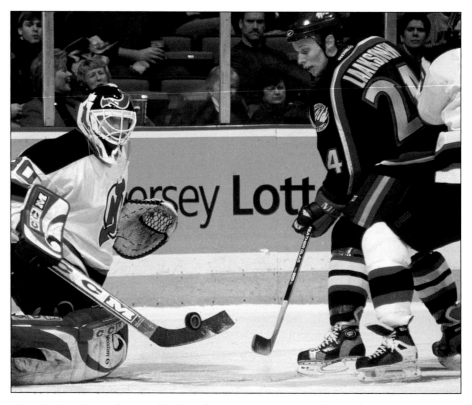

Martin Brodeur, the goalie for the New Jersey Devils hockey team, has been nominated three times as a finalist for the Best Goaltender award.

Atlantic City's Around the Island Marathon Swim is a 22.5-mile course around Absecon Island, in the cold waters of the Atlantic Ocean.

The Atlantic Ocean is a popular destination for swimmers and boaters. Every year, swimmers brave the chilly ocean waters to take part in Atlantic City's Around the Island Marathon Swim. The Atlantic Ocean provides a wide variety of fish to catch. Fishing in New Jersey streams and rivers is also popular.

For those who prefer to stay on land, New Jersey's golf courses and ski areas provide plenty of outdoor recreation. New Jersey is also a great place for horse lovers. The state is home to the United States Equestrian Team, based in Gladstone. Each June, spectators can watch the nation's best horse riders at Gladstone's Festival of Champions.

QUICK FACTS

Hikers and campers can enjoy the outdoors in New Jersey's 300,000 acres of state parks and 4,000 freshwater lakes and streams.

In 1869, New Brunswick hosted the first intercollegiate football game. The game saw Rutgers College defeat Princeton University with a score of 6 to 4.

Non-professional teams include independent baseball teams, such as the Newark Bears and the Somerset Patriots. Both play in their own local ballparks.

Golf has become the most popular seasonal recreational activity in New Jersey. There are more than 211 landscaped golf courses to choose from.

Brain Teasers

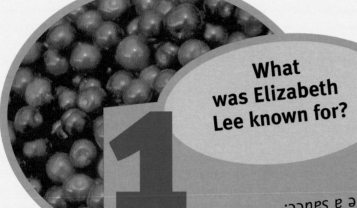

1

What was Elizabeth Lee known for?

Answer: Elizabeth Lee was the first person to make cranberry sauce. Knowing that no one wanted to buy blemished cranberries, she threw them into a pot, boiled them, and made a sauce.

2

Which well-known comic was fired from a job in Atlantic City because people thought he lacked humor?

a. Ed Sullivan

b. Jackie Gleason

c. Red Skelton

d. Johnny Carson

Answer: b. Jackie Gleason. A few years later, he launched a hilarious television program, called *The Honeymooners*.

3

What happened in the Passaic River in 1898?

Answer: John P. Holland launched the first submarine equipped with both a gasoline engine and an electric motor. Holland made several passes up and down the river before returning to shore.

4

What happened on January 9, 1793, in the state of New Jersey?

Answer: Jean-Pierre Blanchard made the first balloon flight in the United States. He delivered a letter to George Washington by hot-air balloon.

5

What flying object spooked the residents of Totowa in 1908?

Answer: William Gary's disk-shaped aircraft, called the "Gary Plane," soared 100 yards at an altitude of only 6 feet. Many towns people thought they had seen a Unidentified Flying Object (UFO).

6

How did a "frog" help end a bitter battle between two New Jersey railroad companies in the late 1800s?

Answer: A "frog," in railroad terms, is a track that crosses over another track. When two railroad companies waged a battle over crossing rights, the army had to be brought in. They installed a "frog," so that the Delaware and Bound Brook Rail Link could cross over the Pennsylvania Railroad line.

7

Would it be difficult to get a burger and fries in New Jersey?

Answer: Probably not. New Jersey has earned the nickname, the "diner capital." It is known for having more diners than anywhere else in the world.

8

What famous board game was originally based on street names in Atlantic City?

Answer: Monopoly, the most popular board game in the world, was created by Charles B. Darrow in 1934.

FOR MORE INFORMATION

Books

Fleming, Thomas J. *New Jersey: A History*. Revised edition. New York: Norton, 1984.

Heide, Robert and John Gilman. *O' New Jersey: Day Tripping, Back Roads, Eateries, and Funky Adventures.* New York: St. Martin's Press, 1992.

Stansfield, Charles A. *New Jersey: A Geography.* Boulder: Westview Press, 1983.

Web sites

You can also go online and have a look at the following Web sites:

New Jersey's Homepage
http://www.state.nj.us

New Jersey Online
http://www.nj.com

50 States: New Jersey
http://www.50states.com/newjerse.htm

Some Web sites stay current longer than others. To find other New Jersey Web sites, enter search terms such as "New Jersey," "Garden State," "Trenton," or any other topic you want to research.

GLOSSARY

archeologists: scientists who study early peoples through artifacts and remains

aviation: relating to flying

commuters: people who travel to and from their jobs in the city, usually by car or train

congregations: groups of people gathered together for worship

descendants: relatives

fertilizer: a substance that is spread over soil to help crops grow

greenhouse: a glass building used to grow plants

immunity: protection from diseases

industrialization: the introduction of manufacturing industries to an area

navigator: a skilled person who directs a moving craft, such as a ship or plane, to its destination

persecuted: to be harassed because of one's religion, race, or beliefs

pharmaceuticals: drugs and medicines used to help cure sickness and disease

population density: the average number of people per unit of area

prehistoric: the period before written history began

proprietors: owners of colonies in North America

rural: relating to the country or countryside, as opposed to the city

segregation: forcing separation and restrictions based on race

Underground Railroad: a system for helping slaves escape

urbanized: a modern city with housing, industries, roads, and a dense population

utility: a public service

INDEX